MEASURING UP
length

Peter Patilla

 Belitha Press

First published in Great Britain in 1999 by

 Belitha Press Limited,
London House, Great Eastern Wharf,
Parkgate Road, London SW11 4NQ

Text copyright © Peter Patilla 1999
Illustrations by Dave Cockcroft

Series editor: Claire Edwards
Editor: Russell Mclean
Series designer: Simeen Karim
Designer: Double Elephant/Rita Wüthrich
Picture researcher: Juliet Duff
Consultant: Martin Hollins

Thanks to Thomas and Joseph Shipman for being the readers; Graham Peacock
of Sheffield Hallam University and Ken Rickwood of Essex University for clarifying
some science ideas; and Alison Patilla for research.

ISBN 1 85561 884 2

Printed in Singapore   9 8 7 6 5 4 3 2 1

British Library Cataloguing in Publication Data
for this book is available from the British Library.

Picture acknowledgements:
Ancient Art and Architecture: 12; **Biro Bic Ltd**: 28; **Bridgeman Art Library**:
5 Giraudon, 8 Victoria & Albert Museum, London, 11 British Library, London,
17 left Giraudon, 18 Index; **Corbis**: 9 Yann Arthus-Bertrand; **Eye Ubiquitous**: 29;
Michael Holford: 10; **Ordnance Survey**: 27 © Crown Copyright Licence Number
MC 88667M0001; **Science and Society Photo Library**: front cover, 7b, 13, 15;
Science Photo Library: 17r Jean-Loup Charmet, 23 left Dr Mitsuo Ohtsuki,
25t & back cover Philippe Plailly; **Tony Stone Images**: 7t, 20, 22, 23r, 25b, 26.

CONTENTS

IN THE BEGINNING

All through history people have found it useful to measure how long things are. The earliest ways of measuring length were quite simple – people used parts of the body, such as hands and feet, as units of length.

palm

One of the most popular body units was the cubit. This was measured as the distance from the elbow to the tip of the outstretched middle finger. Early builders in Egypt and Babylon used the cubit as one of their main units of length. The length of a cubit varied from place to place, but on average it equalled about 50 centimetres.

cubit

Palms

A palm is the width of four closed fingers, not including the thumb. A hand is a little longer, because the measurement includes the thumb. A span is defined as the distance from the tip of the little finger to the tip of the thumb with fingers spread out.

span

Fingers

The unit of a digit or finger was used when measuring small objects. A digit measurement is the width of the forefinger across the first joint.

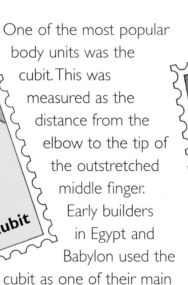
digit

Feet

At first a foot was the distance from the heel to the toe. A pace or stride was a measure of longer distances. People paced out a distance, trying to keep each pace the same size.

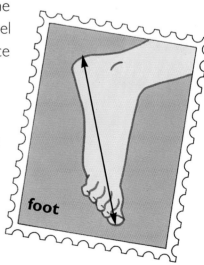
foot

In the Bible, Noah was told to build an ark that was 300 cubits long, 50 cubits wide and 30 cubits tall.

Did you know?
The deepest part of the Pacific Ocean is the Marianas Trench. It is about 6000 fathoms (11 000 metres) deep. If you dropped a metal ball from a boat, it would take more than an hour to reach the sea floor.

Fathoms

The distance from fingertip to fingertip with arms outstretched is called a fathom. This unit was used by sailors to measure the depth of water. They would lower a weighted rope over the side of the boat and count how many fathoms of rope they used before it hit the bottom. The name comes from an old English word, *faethmian*, which means to use both arms. Fathoms are still used sometimes to measure depths under the sea.

Length fact
In the USA, when the navigator of a paddle steamer sounds a depth of 1 fathom, he shouts 'Mark one'. At 2 fathoms, he cries 'Mark twain'. A writer was so fond of these boats that he changed his name to Mark Twain. His best known book is *The Adventures of Huckleberry Finn*.

EARLY STANDARD UNITS

The problem with using parts of the body as measures of length is that people are different sizes – so these units were never very accurate.

Over the years people tried to sort out the confusion over different-sized body lengths. They began to agree on the length of certain units. These standard units made measuring more accurate for people who lived, worked and traded together. Among the first people to develop accurate units were the Egyptians. Their standards date back to about 3000 BC.

Royal cubits

These Egyptian units were based on the digit, palm, span and cubit. A standard royal master cubit was first made from black granite. This was 7 palms long and divided into 28 main sections, each of 1 digit. Some of these digit sections were divided up further. These little divisions meant that for the first time people could measure lengths very accurately. Then all the cubit sticks used throughout Egypt had to be matched against the royal standard.

Length fact

Egyptian children learned that:

1 cubit	=	7 palms
1 small cubit	=	6 palms
1 small span	=	3 palms
1 large span	=	3½ palms
1 palm	=	4 digits
1 hand	=	5 digits

16
1 2 3 4 5 6 7 8 9 10 11 12 13 14 15 16 17 18 19 20 21 22
13 12 11 10 9 8 7 6 5 4 3 2 1

Babylonian cubits

About 4000 years ago the Babylonians also used the cubit, sometimes called a kus, as a unit of length. The Babylonian cubit was also divided into smaller units, each called a shusi. There were 30 shusi in a cubit.

Chinese lengths

Parts of the body were used as measuring units in Ancient China too. The distance from the pulse in the wrist to the base of the thumb was used for short lengths. Units with the same name varied in length from region to region, and for different uses. Stonemasons and carpenters all had their own sizes of unit.

The chih and the chang

In 221 BC Emperor Shih Huang Ti ordered that two basic measures called the chih and the chang should be used as standard units. In today's measurements, the chih would be about 25 centimetres long and the chang about 3 metres long. Like most Chinese units, these were then divided into ten smaller sections.

Egyptian builders working on the pyramids at Giza used cubit sticks to work out their measurements with great precision. The four sides of the Great Pyramid are accurate to within a few centimetres of each other, even though they are more than 230 metres long.

The Egyptians made beautiful and very accurate tools for measuring length, such as this stone cubit stick.

Did you know?
The oldest standard unit of length dates from about 2100 BC. It was based on the statue of the ruler Gudea of Lagash (in modern-day Iraq). The foot of the statue is about 26 centimetres long and is divided into 16 parts.

INVADERS AND TRADERS

Through invasions and the spread of trade, the Greeks and then the Romans influenced how length was measured throughout Europe.

The Greeks and the Romans spread across Europe, Africa and western Asia between about 1000 BC and 400 AD. Wherever they went they used their own units of length, which became the basis for local systems in different parts of the world. The main Greek lengths were the finger, the foot and the Olympic cubit. There were 16 fingers in a foot and 24 fingers in a cubit. The Roman units included the foot, the pace and the rod.

Charlemagne's foot

The Roman units of length were still used throughout Europe in the Middle Ages. But these units had changed over time and from country to country. In 789 AD the Emperor of Europe, Charlemagne, ordered everyone to use the royal foot (the length of his own foot) as the standard length. But despite his efforts most people carried on using the units they were used to.

Trading standards

During the Middle Ages people travelled across Europe to buy and sell goods at huge trade fairs. To avoid cheating, every trader had to use standard units of length. The ell was a very important unit, because it was used to measure cloth, a valuable item at that time. In some countries an ell was the distance between the elbows with arms outstretched. But in Holland it was the distance between bent elbows with the hands clenched and touching on the chest. To avoid confusion, at trade fairs in the Champagne region of France every ell stick was checked against a standard iron bar about 76 centimetres long.

The Emperor Charlemagne (742–814 AD)

Traders at the Champagne fairs had to check their lengths of cloth against the iron standard held by the Keeper of the Fair.

Explorers to America

In the 1500s Europeans sailed to America and began to settle there. They brought their own systems of measuring, and these spread to the American colonies too. Modern American measures, called US customary units, are based on these early European units of length.

Did you know?
One of the oldest units of length was called a stadium. It was the length of the original racetrack at Olympia, in Ancient Greece. This was about 192 metres long.

Fingers and nails

Fingers and nails were important measures in the clothmaking industry too. A finger was defined as 4½ inches (about 11 centimetres). Some people measured a nail from the tip of the middle finger to the second knuckle, which was half a finger. Others measured it across the four nails with fingers closed. The hems on cloaks were usually one nail wide – about 2¼ inches.

The site of the race-track at Olympia in Greece.

MEASURING THE LAND

When people farmed, they needed to know exactly how much land they owned. Most of the units they invented are no longer used, but the names remain in our language even today.

The Egyptians were among the first people to use chains and knotted ropes to measure their land. Every year the River Nile would flood and wash away markers at the edges of the fields. After the flood, farmers needed to measure out the land again as accurately as possible. Later, in about 300 BC, the Greeks used knotted floating lines to measure their coastline.

Did you know?
We no longer use the chain – except on the cricket pitch. The length of the wicket is exactly 1 chain (22 yards, or about 20 metres).

Gunter's chain

In the seventeenth century an English mathematician called Edmund Gunter devised a special chain made up of 100 links. This was exactly 22 yards long. Gunter's chain was such an accurate instrument for measuring land that it was used by farmers and surveyors until the middle of the twentieth century.

This Egyptian painting on the wall of a tomb shows farmers measuring a field of corn with a knotted rope.

Rods

Rods were one of the earliest and most important standard units of length for measuring land. Later they also came to be known as poles or perches. There were originally ten Roman feet in a rod. Over time the rod grew to a length of 5½ yards (5 metres). In the Middle Ages a rod was worked out by lining up 16 men outside church on a Sunday morning and measuring the total length of their left feet. From the sixteenth century onwards there were 4 rods in a chain.

Furlongs

A furlong was defined as the distance a team of oxen could plough a furrow before they needed to rest. The name comes from the phrase 'furrow long'. It measured 220 yards (about 201 metres), so there were exactly 8 furlongs in a mile. During the Middle Ages furlongs were mainly used to measure round the edge of a field. Today furlongs are still used to measure horse racecourses.

Leagues

A league was a long unit used by the Greeks in the first centuries AD. The name league was taken from the Ancient Gauls, who lived in Northern Europe from around 400 BC. An English league equalled 3 miles.

This scene shows oxen ploughing a furrow in about 1050 AD. The phrase 'furrow long' became shortened to furlong.

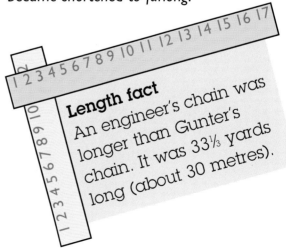

Length fact
An engineer's chain was longer than Gunter's chain. It was 33⅓ yards long (about 30 metres).

FEET AND INCHES

For hundreds of years the most common units used to measure short distances were feet and inches. These have now mostly been replaced by the metric system, but they are still used in some parts of the world, such as the USA.

This mosaic was made in about the fourth century AD. It shows the spirit of creation, called Ktisis, holding a Roman foot ruler.

An emperor's standard

To make sure that a foot was always the same length, the Romans made copper bars to be used as standard units. The length of the bars probably matched the foot size of a Roman emperor. Each bar was divided into twelve equal parts. The Roman word for a twelfth was *uncia*. This gave us the English word inch.

The Greeks and the Romans both used the foot as a unit of length. People had been using their feet as a rough measuring unit for thousands of years, but a widely-used standard unit was not made until Greek times. The feet and inches used in modern times are based on a system introduced by the Romans, whose standard foot was shorter than the Greek foot. The Romans were the first people to divide the foot into 12 smaller units of equal length.

Length fact
The word ounce also comes from the Roman *uncia*. This is because Roman copper foot bars weighed 1 pound. In earlier times there were 12 ounces in a pound.

The line at the bottom of this marble tablet is a Roman or Greek foot measure. The tablet was made in about 300 AD.

Confusion rules

During the Middle Ages Roman feet and inches were not used everywhere in Europe. In about 1150 King David I of Scotland defined the inch as the distance across a man's thumb at the base of the nail. But about 200 years later King Edward II of England decided that, 'The length of an inch shall be equal to three grains of barley, dry and round, placed end to end lengthwise.' So all through the Middle Ages you could never be sure of the exact length of feet and inches from one country to the next.

British and US inches

Until 1959 the length of a British and an American inch was fractionally different. The US inch equalled 25.40005 millimetres, while the British inch was slightly shorter, equal to 25.39998 millimetres. Although the difference between the two inches was very small, it made things very difficult for aircraft engineers who discovered that American nuts did not quite fit British bolts. After years of confusion, it was finally agreed that a standard inch should be defined as exactly 25.4 millimetres.

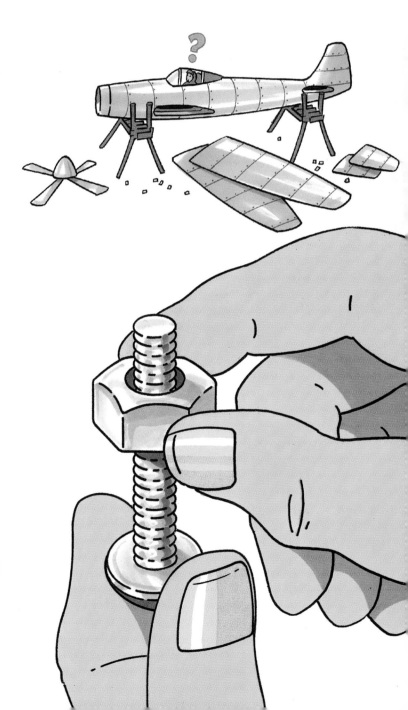

MILES AND YARDS

Long distances were often measured in miles and yards. But miles were not always divided into yards – this happened gradually over centuries.

As the centuries passed, people needed to measure long distances more and more accurately. To help them the mile was divided into 8 furlongs. Eventually these in turn were divided into yards. This slow, haphazard way of dividing up is why there are such an odd number of yards in a mile today.

Length fact
Today there are 3 feet in a yard and 1760 yards in a mile, although countries have not always agreed about this. The old Swedish mile was almost 11 000 yards long!

A thousand paces

We have the Romans to thank for the mile as a unit of length. The Roman pace was a double step, about 5 feet (1.5 metres) in length. It was commonly used as a measuring unit. When the Romans marched across the countries they conquered, they counted out every thousand paces. The Roman phrase for this distance was *mille passus*, from which we get our word mile. We can tell from the hundreds of Roman milestones scattered across Europe that the Roman mile was shorter than the one we use today. Romans didn't use yards, but if they had, there would only have been 1618 yards in one of their miles.

A royal yardstick

In northern Europe a yard was the length of a girdle worn by the Anglo-Saxons. In European countries further south it was a double cubit, which made it about 1 metre long. Like most measuring units, yards varied over time and from place to place. In the 1100s King Henry I of England decided that a yard should be the distance from his nose to the thumb of his outstretched arm. Because this early yardstick was based on the arm length of the king, miles, yards, feet and inches became known as imperial measures. In 1215 King John gave orders that a standard iron yard should measure 3 feet, each of 12 inches, 'neither more nor less'.

Measuring in public

Yardsticks were often used as measuring instruments, but as these became worn down, they had to be checked regularly for accuracy. Bronze plaques showing a yard were displayed in town squares so that craftworkers and traders could check the accuracy of their own measures.

The Standard Imperial Yard

After centuries of uncertainty over the length of the yard, in 1760 it was decided that Britain needed one standard measure. But the original Standard Imperial Yard was lost when the Houses of Parliament were destroyed by fire in 1834. A new standard, created in 1855, was kept in a fire-proof lead case, buried in the walls of the new parliament building. Every 20 years the wall was unbricked and the standard yard checked for accuracy.

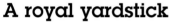

This Elizabethan standard yardstick is made of bronze. It dates back to around 1582.

METRIC MEASUREMENTS

The metre is the basic unit of the metric system. The name comes from the Greek word *metron*, which means a measure.

A decimal system of length (one based on the number ten) was first suggested in 1670 by a French vicar, Gabriel Mouton. But his idea was not fully developed until the 1790s, during the French Revolution. The Revolution was a time of change, and the new government demanded a fair measuring system for its people. Scientists wanted a unit that would not change over time or from place to place. So they decided to base the new system not on the human body, but on the dimensions of the Earth.

Delambre and Méchain

The scientists declared that the new metre would equal the distance between the North Pole and the Equator divided by ten million. But how to measure that distance? The problem was solved by two engineers, Jean Delambre and Pierre Méchain. They decided to measure the distance between Dunkirk and Barcelona and then use mathematics to calculate the whole distance from the North Pole to the Equator. They did not have to measure every step of the way, but used their knowledge of angles to work out distances as they went along. Their journey began in 1792. Seven years later they reached Barcelona and finally calculated the length of the metre.

Did you know?
Delambre and Méchain were often arrested on suspicion of being spies. People thought they were signalling to enemy forces with their flags and poles!

For all people, for all time

Charles-Maurice de Talleyrand was a clever politician who kept his head through the French Revolution, even though he belonged to an aristocratic family. In 1790 he launched an important debate about weights and measures. The French Academy of Sciences adopted the metric system nine years later, with the motto 'For all people, for all time'.

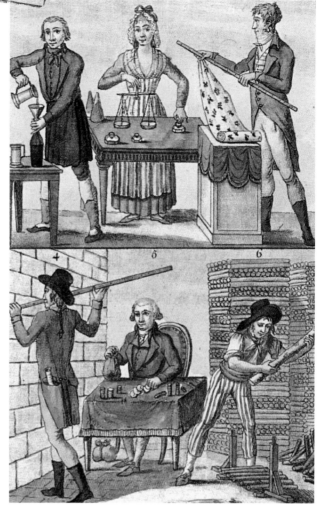

Charles-Maurice de Talleyrand (1754–1838)

These pictures from 1800 showed how to use the new metric measures introduced during the French Revolution.

Europe goes metric

After the French Revolution Napoleon Bonaparte ruled France. He conquered many European countries too. Although people often continued to use their own measuring units, the metric system slowly spread across Europe. Today most countries use this system for everyday measuring. Some countries, such as Britain, use a mixture of old imperial measurements and newer metric ones. Scientists and engineers all over the world use metric measures.

Length fact

Working with numbers that can be divided by ten makes life very simple.

10 millimetres	= 1 centimetre
10 centimetres	= 1 decimetre
10 decimetres	= 1 metre
1000 metres	= 1 kilometre

MEASURING INSTRUMENTS

From very early times people have invented and designed special instruments to help them measure more accurately and easily.

The first measuring tools were simple rulers, sticks and tapes, which have not changed much over the ages. Egyptian masons used a wooden ruler with a bevelled (sloping) edge. Two left-hand palms were pictured on the ruler, each palm divided into digits. Over the years people have used cubit sticks, rods, yardsticks and metre sticks to check length. In the Middle Ages plain rulers with no markings at all were sold. Users probably made their own divisions, depending on what they were measuring. Rulers used in schools today are usually 30 centimetres or 12 inches long.

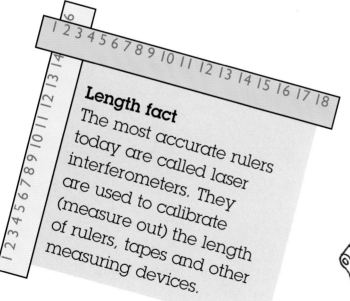

Length fact
The most accurate rulers today are called laser interferometers. They are used to calibrate (measure out) the length of rulers, tapes and other measuring devices.

Fifteenth-century stonemasons (above) used dividers to check the sizes of the stones they built churches with.

A micrometer (left) is used to measure tiny lengths like the thickness of paper.

Folding rulers

The Romans invented folding rulers so that people could measure long lengths using an instrument that could be easily carried. They were 6 or 12 inches long and made of bronze. These pocket rulers were used by officials rather than craftworkers, who would have found them too expensive. Folding rulers disappeared with the Romans, and did not reappear until the seventeenth century. The folding rulers we use today are usually a yard or a metre long.

Dividers

It is not known quite when dividers were invented, but they were used by the Greeks and the Romans. Dividers have straight legs, often with points at each end, and are used to compare, transfer or mark off lengths. For example, if you are planning a walking holiday on a map, you might aim to walk 20 kilometres every day. Using the map scale, you set the dividers to that distance. Then you can easily mark off equal sized steps along your route. Each step would be one day's walking. Ever since the first maps were drawn up, sailors have used dividers for marking off distances on their charts to help them navigate the oceans.

Callipers

Callipers were invented thousands of years ago. They have curved legs and are used to measure lengths that are difficult to check with a ruler or tape. You can use callipers to measure the length of an egg or a ball. Once the legs are the right distance apart, the the measurement can easily be read from a ruler.

Trundle wheels

Surveyors use trundle wheels to measure long distances. Each time the wheel makes one revolution (a complete turn), a counter records the distance that it has travelled. Cars have a similar instrument called an odometer. This shows the distance of a journey in kilometres.

LENGTHS AND DIMENSIONS

Length is a measure of how long something is, but we also use units of length in other ways – to describe the size of an object for example.

The dimensions of an object tell us its size. The words most often used to describe dimensions are length (A), width or breadth (B), and height (C). Sometimes these words are confusing. A telegraph pole standing upright may be 5 metres tall, but lying on the ground it will be 5 metres long. Width (or breadth) is the measurement of an object from one side to the other. The distance through the middle of an object is its thickness.

Tallness and height

Tallness and height are both vertical measurements. Tallness describes the length of something standing upright, such as a building or a person. Height is the distance of an object from the ground or from sea level. So a girl might be 90 centimetres tall, but if she climbed a tree she could be 3 metres high. In everyday speech we often use both words to mean the same thing.

The world's highest mountain is Mount Everest (left) in the Himalayas, which is 8848 metres high. The tallest mountain is Mauna Kea, on Hawaii. It is 10 205 metres tall. Most of this is below sea level, leaving only 4205 metres above the water.

Distance

Distance is how far apart two points are. We talk about the length of a pen, but the distance between two towns. Distance is often measured 'as the crow flies' – meaning in a straight line. But it is often impossible to travel between two places in a straight line. The winding roads mean that your journey will be longer than the distance as the crow flies. So it is often more useful to describe the actual distance travelled.

Depth

The word depth is used in two ways. The depth of water describes the vertical distance from the surface to the bottom. We might also talk about the depth of a cave – this means how far back the cave stretches, but not how far down it goes.

Perimeter

The length around the edge of an object is called its perimeter. If the object is circular its perimeter is called the circumference. Hat, collar and waist sizes are the circumferences of parts of the body. Girth is an old English word meaning the distance around the waist.

Did you know?
There are about 96 000 kilometres of tubes carrying blood around your body – long enough to stretch around the circumference of Earth an amazing 2½ times.

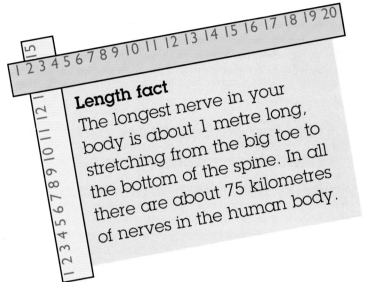

Length fact
The longest nerve in your body is about 1 metre long, stretching from the big toe to the bottom of the spine. In all there are about 75 kilometres of nerves in the human body.

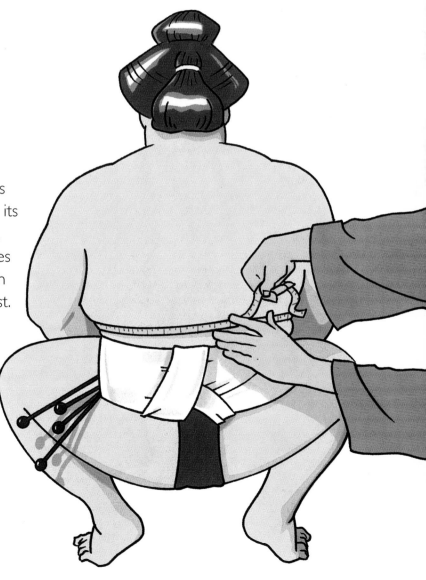

LONG AND SHORT UNITS

From the earliest times astronomers and scientists wanted to measure lengths that would help them understand the Universe.

The Ancient Greeks were among the first people to study the distances of space. Some of the lengths used by scientists and astronomers today are too huge to imagine. Others are so short you cannot see them.

The first person known to have calculated the Earth's circumference was a Greek, Eratosthenes, who lived in the third century BC. Over the ages other great astronomers, such as Copernicus, calculated the distances of space ever more accurately. Scientists today have devised special units for very short and very long lengths. Modern space exploration relies on these units to make calculations that are as accurate as humanly possible.

Length fact

A light year is a unit of measurement used to describe incredibly long distances in space. It is defined as the distance light waves travel through space in one year – about 9460 billion kilometres.

Microscopic lengths

Scientists have developed the metric system to include small and microscopic lengths. The units they use are shown below.

metre	1 m
decimetre	0.1 m
centimetre	0.01 m
millimetre	0.001 m
micrometre	0.000 001 m
nanometre	0.000 000 001 m
picometre	0.000 000 000 001 m
femtometre	0.000 000 000 000 001 m
attometre	0.000 000 000 000 000 001 m

Viruses and atoms

Can you imagine how small an attometre is, or what all those zeros after the decimal point really mean? The thickness of one page of this book is about 0.000125 metres, or 125 micrometres. Viruses, which give you illnesses such as flu, are microscopically small. They are about 1 micrometre in length. But atoms are even tinier. They are less than 1 nanometre long.

Astronomic lengths

Scientists also use metric units to measure large and astronomic lengths.

metre	1 m
decametre	10 m
hectometre	100 m
kilometre	1000 m
miriametre	10 000 m
megametre	1 000 000 m
gigametre	1 000 000 000 m
terrametre	1 000 000 000 000 m

The longest unit of all

One of the brightest stars in the sky is called Antares. It is about 3 800 000 000 000 000 kilometres from Earth. This distance is equal to 3.8 million terrametres, or about 400 light years. The parsec is one of the longest units used by scientists. It equals 3.26 light years. Even this is not long enough sometimes, so they use kiloparsecs (one thousand parsecs) and even megaparsecs (one million parsecs). These units help astronomers make incredibly complex calculations about distances in space.

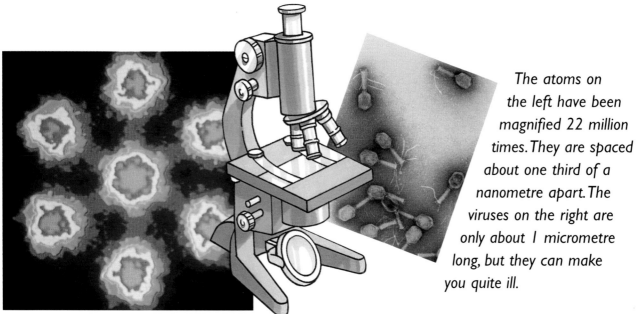

The atoms on the left have been magnified 22 million times. They are spaced about one third of a nanometre apart. The viruses on the right are only about 1 micrometre long, but they can make you quite ill.

MEASURING WITH WAVES

Today scientists are able to measure difficult lengths by using radio, sound and light waves. These allow them to measure with more accuracy than ever before.

Radar uses radio waves to measure distance. The system was first developed in the 1930s by an Englishman, Sir Robert Watson-Watt. Radio waves are sent out from a revolving dish. An echo is reflected back by any object that the waves hit, such as a plane or ship. The echo is picked up by the dish and sent to a computer that works out the distance and direction of the object.

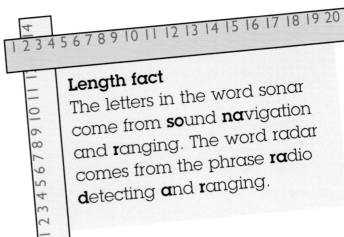

Length fact
The letters in the word sonar come from **so**und **na**vigation and **r**anging. The word radar comes from the phrase **ra**dio **d**etecting **a**nd **r**anging.

Sound waves

Sound can be used to measure distances underwater, such as the depth of the sea or the distance to an underwater object such as a submarine or a shoal of fish. This system was developed in 1915 by a French scientist, Professor Paul Langevin. Pulses of sound are sent out by the ship, they hit any object in their path and bounce back to the ship rather like an echo. A special instrument measures the time this takes and works out how far the sound pulses have travelled. In the past these instruments were called fathometers, because depth used to be measured in fathoms. Today they are known as sonar devices or echo sounders.

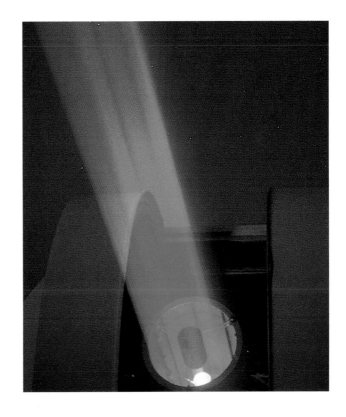

The picture below shows a radar screen at an airport. Air traffic controllers use radar to check the positions of all the planes circling around the airport.

A laser beam is fired from a telescope in France (right). The beam is measuring the distance from the Earth to the Moon.

Light waves

Scientists now use light waves to measure both long and short distances with great accuracy. Light waves are sent out from a laser and are bounced off any object in their path. A computer measures how long the light waves take to return, which allows it to calculate how far away the object is. The first astronauts to the Moon placed a special mirror there called a LIDAR (**li**ght ra**dar**). This device can measure the huge distances from the Moon to Earth (on average 384 000 kilometres) to an accuracy of a few centimetres. It is also used to measure the distance between any two places on our planet.

Standard metre

The original standard metre was a metal bar, but since 1983 light waves have been used to define the length of the standard metre as accurately as possible.

MAPS AND SCALES

If you are using a map, you need to know about scales. Imagine how large a map would be if it was drawn full size.

An aerial view of the River Amazon. The distances are small if you measure them on this page. In fact the section of the river shown here measures several kilometres.

Length fact
Map makers scratch figures called bench marks on to walls and monuments. They show the height of the land at that point above sea level and are used to map contours accurately.

Looking at a map of a village, city or country is rather like looking at a long distance photograph taken from a great height. This is because when things are drawn to scale on a map, the actual distances are scaled down so that they will fit on a sheet of paper. Different maps have different scales, depending on how big the actual area is and how much detail needs to be shown. A large scale shows a small area in a lot of detail. A road map of a town or a city might use a large scale to show every single street. A small scale shows a greater area but less detail. This type of map would be very useful if you wanted to plan a long motorway journey of hundreds of kilometres.

These maps show the same area using different scales. As the scale gets larger you see less area but more detail, rather like zooming down from above.

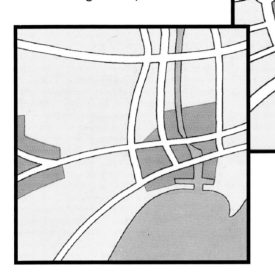

What does 1:50 000 mean?

To measure a real distance from a map, you need to know the exact scale of the map. A scale of 1:50 000 means that one unit of length on the map represents 50 000 of the same unit on the ground. So a road that is 1 centimetre long on the map is 50 000 centimetres long in reality. This equals 500 metres, or half a kilometre. In this way drivers using a road map can make a rough estimate of the actual length of their journey.

Measuring with wheels

For making accurate measurements from a map, a small version of the trundle wheel can be used. You set the scale of the map on a dial and then push the wheel along the chosen route. The wheel converts the distance it travels in centimetres into the real journey distance in kilometres.

Contours

Contour lines on a map show mountains, hills and valleys. Each line has a number marked on it – this is the height of the land above sea level in metres or feet. Everywhere along one line is the same height. Walkers and cyclists use such maps to work out how hard their route will be. Lines close together show steep land. Contours far apart show a gentle slope.

When the contour lines on a map are close together like this, the land is very steep.

COMPARING LENGTHS

Nowadays Britain uses the metric system for measuring length. But people still find it useful to compare metric and imperial units.

Very small lengths are measured in millimetres or fractions of an inch. A comparison is that 6 millimetres is about the same as ¼ inch. A grain of rice is about this long. Short lengths are measured in centimetres or inches. One inch equals about 2.5 centimetres. The width of an adult's thumb across the joint is usually about 1 inch.

An average pen is about 15 centimetres or 6 inches long. You can measure more accurately using millimetres. This pen is 150 millimetres long.

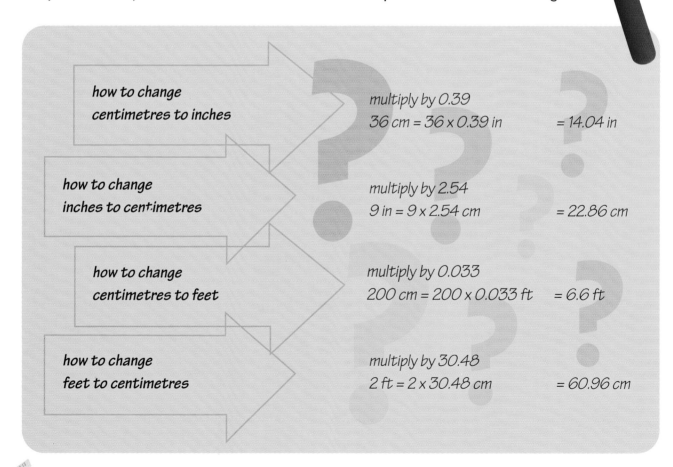

how to change
centimetres to inches

multiply by 0.39
36 cm = 36 x 0.39 in   *= 14.04 in*

how to change
inches to centimetres

multiply by 2.54
9 in = 9 x 2.54 cm   *= 22.86 cm*

how to change
centimetres to feet

multiply by 0.033
200 cm = 200 x 0.033 ft   *= 6.6 ft*

how to change
feet to centimetres

multiply by 30.48
2 ft = 2 x 30.48 cm   *= 60.96 cm*

Metres, yards and feet

Longer distances, such as the length of a garden or a golf course, can be measured in metres, feet or yards. One metre is about the same as 3¼ feet, which is a little bit longer than 1 yard. The height of an inside door is usually 2 metres, or about 6½ feet.

Kilometres and miles

Really long lengths, such as the distance between two towns, are measured in kilometres or miles. A mile is longer than a kilometre. A useful comparison is that 5 miles is about equal to 8 kilometres. At a steady pace, most people can walk about 3 miles or 5 kilometres in one hour.

A large bus like this is about 12 metres or 13 yards long. The distance the bus travels is measured in kilometres or miles.

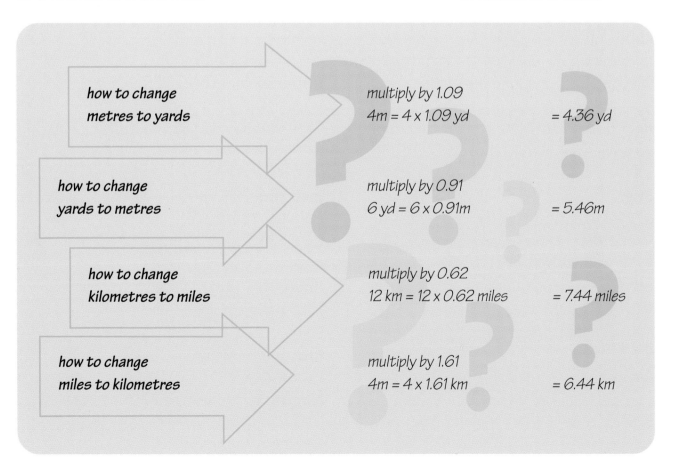

how to change metres to yards	multiply by 1.09 4m = 4 x 1.09 yd	= 4.36 yd
how to change yards to metres	multiply by 0.91 6 yd = 6 x 0.91m	= 5.46m
how to change kilometres to miles	multiply by 0.62 12 km = 12 x 0.62 miles	= 7.44 miles
how to change miles to kilometres	multiply by 1.61 4m = 4 x 1.61 km	= 6.44 km

LENGTHY WORDS

centimetre (cm) A metric unit of length. There are 100 centimetres in 1 metre.

chain An old English unit of 22 yards (about 20 metres), used for measuring land.

chang An ancient Chinese unit, equalling about 3 metres.

chih An ancient Chinese unit, equal to about 25 centimetres.

circumference The length around the edge of a circular object, such as the Earth.

cubit An old unit, defined as the distance from the elbow to the tip of the middle finger, equal to about 50 centimetres.

decimetre (dm) A metric unit, equalling 10 centimetres. Ten decimetres equal 1 metre.

digit An old unit, defined as the width of the forefinger across the first joint. Sometimes called a **finger**.

ell The distance from elbow to elbow with fists touching the chest. The ell was used to measure cloth in the Middle Ages.

fathom A unit equal to 6 feet, used to measure the depth of water. It was defined as the distance between the fingertips with arms outstretched.

finger Another name for a **digit**.

foot (ft) An imperial unit. Originally the foot was simply the length from heel to toe. Today it is defined as a length of 12 inches (about 30 centimetres).

furlong An old unit of 220 yards (about 201 metres). There are 8 furlongs in a mile.

girth The distance around a person's waist.

hand A unit measured across the thumb and four closed fingers (4 inches). Hands are still used today to measure the height of horses.

imperial measures Common units of length used in Britain before metric lengths were introduced. They include miles, yards, feet and inches.

inch (in) An imperial unit. The name comes from the Roman word *uncia*, meaning one twelfth. There are 12 inches in 1 foot.

kilometre (km) A metric unit. There are 1000 metres in a kilometre.

kus The Babylonian name for a cubit.

league An old unit, equal to 3 miles in Britain and the USA. In France a league was 4 kilometres long.

light year A unit used to measure huge distances in space. It is defined as the distance light travels through space in one year – about 9460 billion kilometres.

metre (m) A metric length. There are 100 centimetres in 1 metre. One thousand metres equals 1 kilometre.

metric system A decimal system of measuring (based on the number ten). The main metric units are millimetres, centimetres, metres and kilometres.

mile An imperial unit. The name comes from the Roman phrase *mille passus* – a thousand paces. Today 1 mile equals 1760 yards.

millimetre (mm) A metric length. There are 10 millimetres in 1 centimetre.

nail An old unit commonly used for measuring cloth. It was the distance from the tip of the middle finger to the second joint, about 2¼ inches (about 5.5 centimetres).

nautical mile A unit for measuring distance at sea. In the UK it is just over 2027 yards. An American nautical mile is 2 yards shorter.

pace The distance of one stride. The Roman pace was a double step of about 5 feet.

palm The distance across the palm with the fingers closed, not including the thumb.

parsec A unit used by scientists and astronomers. It is equal to 3.26 light years.

perch Another name for a **rod**.

perimeter The distance measured around the edge of an object.

pole Another name for a **rod**.

rod An old measure of 5½ yards (about 5 metres) which was used to measure land. Sometimes called a **perch** or a **pole**.

royal foot A unit which matched the foot length of Emperor Charlemagne.

royal master cubit In Ancient Egypt, this was the standard cubit length.

shusi An ancient unit equal to one thirtieth of a Babylonian cubit.

span The distance from the tip of the little finger to the tip of the thumb with fingers outstretched.

stadium An ancient Greek unit, equal to about 192 metres.

standard lengths Lengths that everyone agrees to use. Imperial, US customary and metric lengths are all standard units of length.

unit A standard measure of something which can represent length, weight or volume.

US customary units The system of lengths used in the USA, based on the British imperial system. They include miles, yards, feet and inches.

yard (yd) An imperial unit, equal to 3 feet. There are 1760 yards in a mile.

INDEX